Also in the *Meet . . .* series

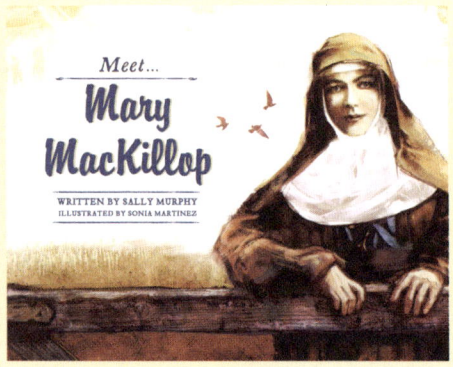

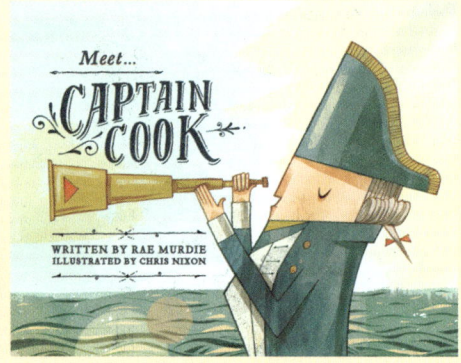

And look out for more *Meet . . .* books coming soon

Meet...

WEARY DUNLOP

WRITTEN BY CLAIRE SAXBY
ILLUSTRATED BY JEREMY LORD

RANDOM HOUSE AUSTRALIA

To Bill, love always. CS

À Claude, parce-que t'y as cru depuis le début. JL

A Random House book
Published by Random House Australia Pty Ltd
Level 3, 100 Pacific Highway, North Sydney NSW 2060
www.randomhouse.com.au

First published by Random House Australia in 2015

Random House Books is part of the Penguin Random House group of companies whose addresses can be found at global.penguinrandomhouse.com.

National Library of Australia
Cataloguing-in-Publication Entry

Creator: Saxby, Claire, author
Title: Meet Weary Dunlop/Claire Saxby; Jeremy Lord, illustrator
ISBN: 978 0 85798 536 1 (hbk)
Series: Meet; 8.
Target Audience: For children.
Subjects: Dunlop, E. E. (Ernest Edward), 1907–1993
Burma–Siam Railroad
Surgeons – Australia – Biography – Juvenile literature
World War, 1939–1945 – Medical care – Juvenile literature
Other Authors/Contributors: Lord, Jeremy, illustrator
Dewey Number: 617.092

Cover and internal design by Kirby Armstrong
Printed and bound in China by RR Donnelley

WEARY DUNLOP

was an Australian Army surgeon during World War II.
This is the story of how Weary's bravery and compassion helped to
save the lives and bolster the spirits of fellow prisoners of war
on the Thai–Burma Railway.

Ernest Edward Dunlop grew up racing around the countryside, exploring and adventuring. There was always plenty of work to be done, but Ernest found time for imagining a world beyond the farm.

At school, Ernest was up for any challenge. He completed four years of secondary school in three, joined the cadets and played sport all year round.

It was at university that Ernest was given his nickname. Dunlop = tyres = tires = weary. Weary the medical student was also a larrikin and champion sportsman, boxing for Victoria and playing rugby for Australia.

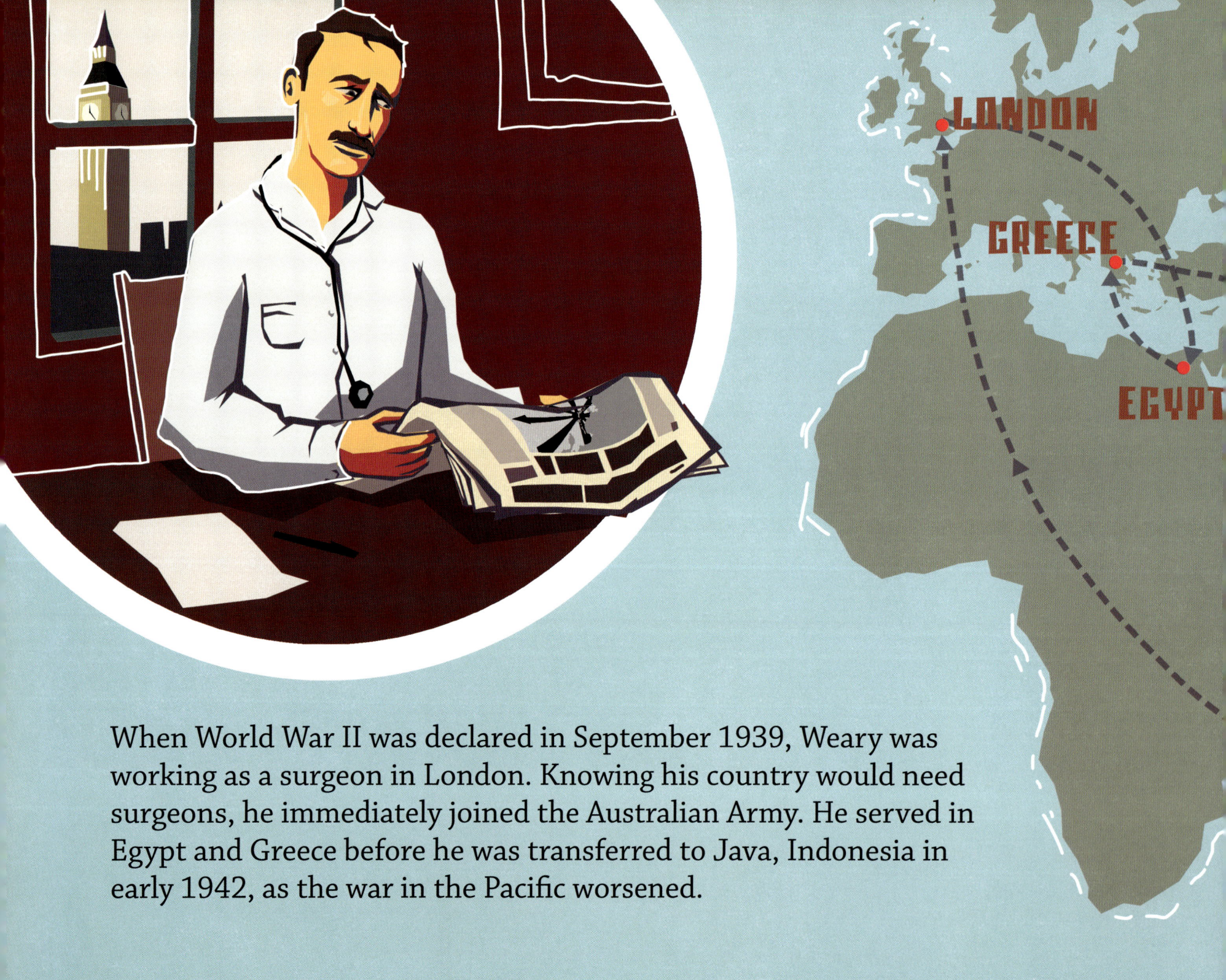

When World War II was declared in September 1939, Weary was working as a surgeon in London. Knowing his country would need surgeons, he immediately joined the Australian Army. He served in Egypt and Greece before he was transferred to Java, Indonesia in early 1942, as the war in the Pacific worsened.

Weary was in charge of a military hospital when the Japanese Army invaded. They fought the Allied forces, which was made up of the British, Australian and Dutch armies. After the Japanese won control of Java, the staff and patients became prisoners of war (POWs).

At the POW camps, Weary was put in command of the British and Australian prisoners. He ordered whatever food and medicine he could through the Japanese guards and sourced extra supplies from people in the Javanese community.

Weary was tall and confident and very skilled both as a surgeon and as a commanding officer. This helped him to negotiate with the Japanese guards. Even so, sometimes he lost his temper and was punished. But always, he protected his men.

Desperate for news of the outside world, the prisoners attempted to smuggle in a radio in a cartload of food. When a guard began to search the cart, Weary swooped in and tucked the radio under his arm. 'Medical supplies,' he said as he strode away.

Discovery would have meant certain death.

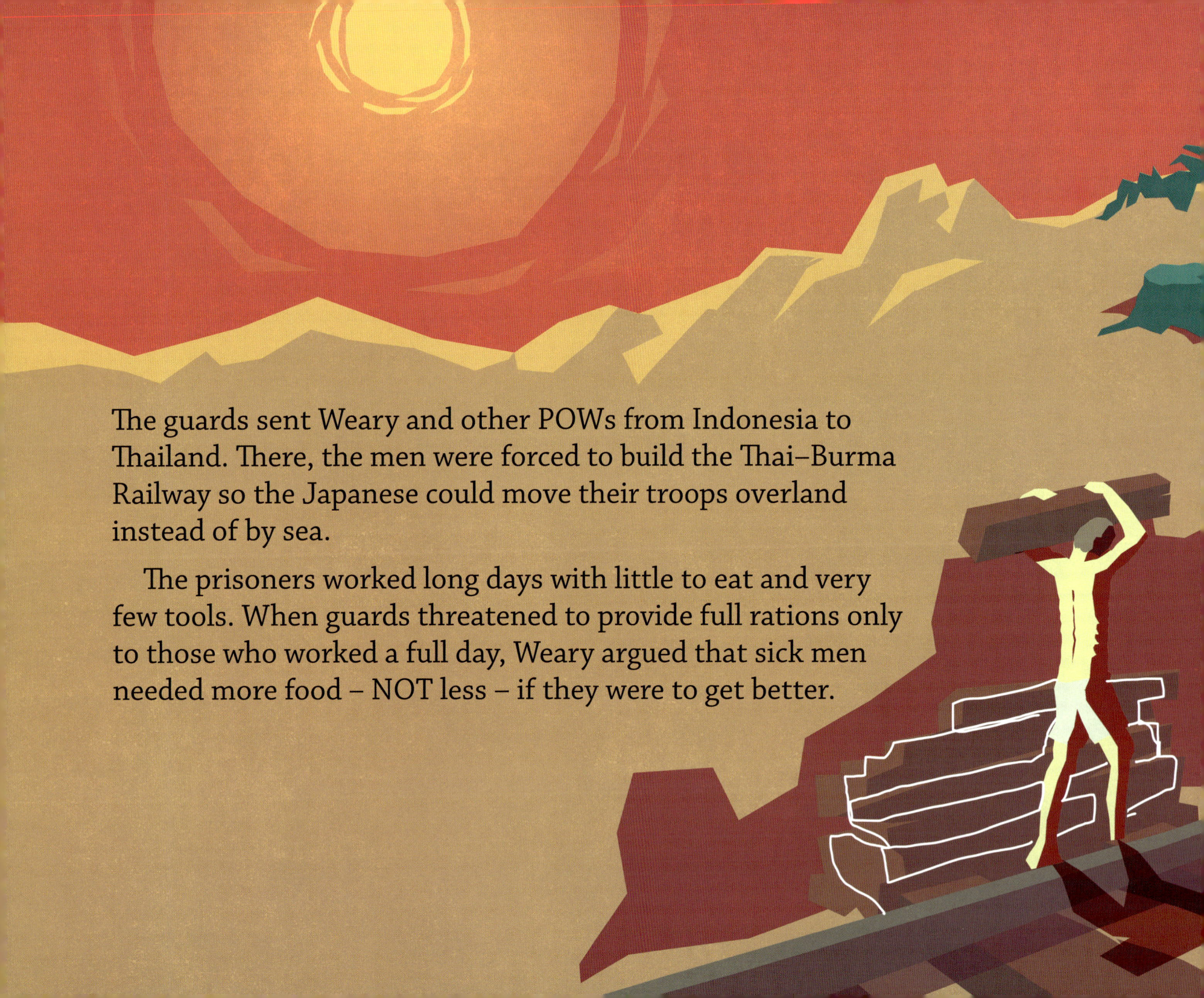

The guards sent Weary and other POWs from Indonesia to Thailand. There, the men were forced to build the Thai–Burma Railway so the Japanese could move their troops overland instead of by sea.

The prisoners worked long days with little to eat and very few tools. When guards threatened to provide full rations only to those who worked a full day, Weary argued that sick men needed more food – NOT less – if they were to get better.

One dark night, Weary performed an emergency operation on a fellow prisoner. It was a difficult procedure in poor conditions but it was successful. The Japanese audience were very impressed.

'You – number one,' said a soldier.

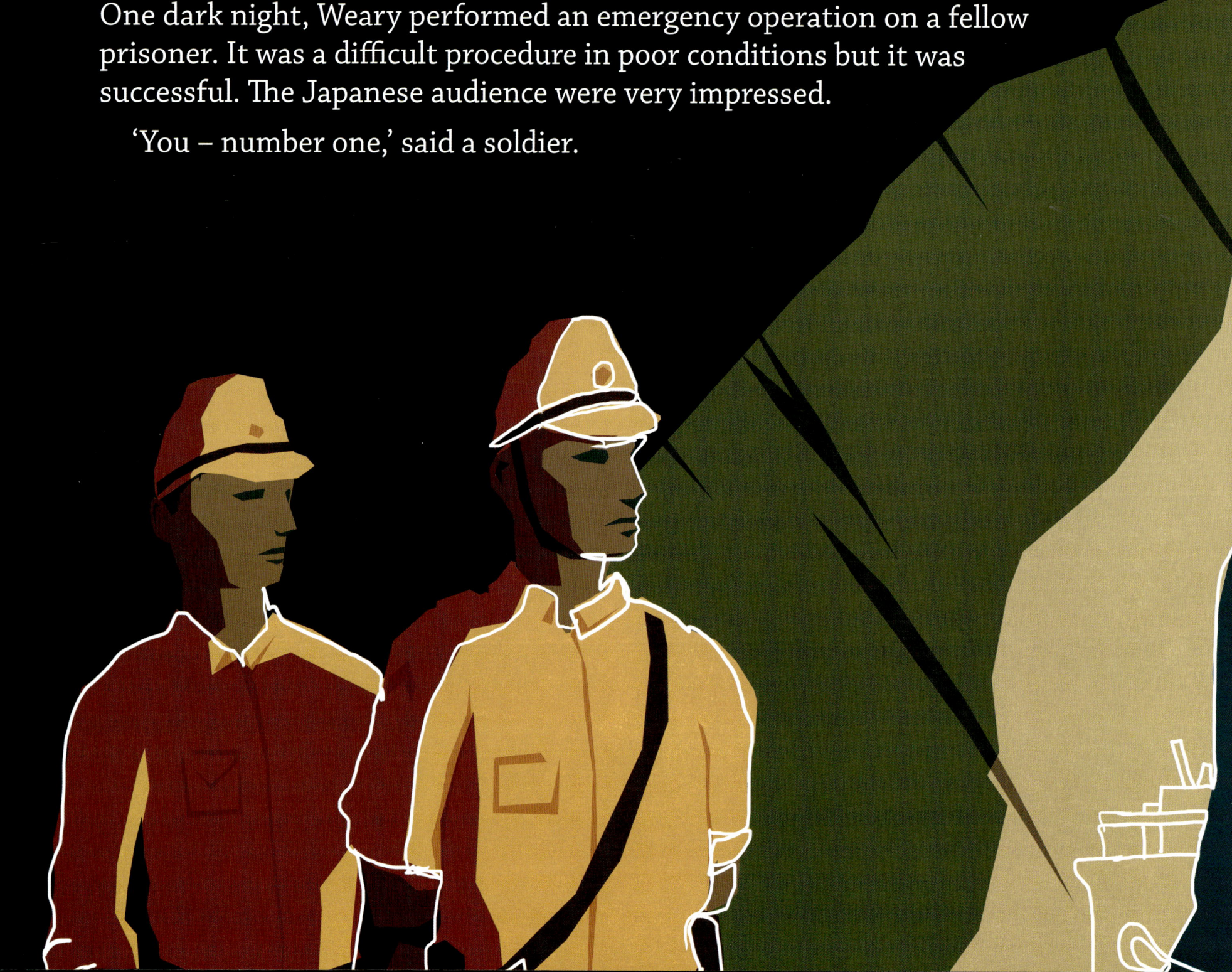

Weary may have won the respect of some guards, but life at the railway camp kept getting worse. He constantly argued with the guards to keep the sick and injured safe until they were well enough to work. This became more difficult when the Japanese Command increased pressure to get the railway finished.

Medical equipment was scarce, but Weary's early days on the farm helped him to make do with what was available. The men made huts and beds from bamboo, as well as water bottles and needles. When the prisoners ran out of ulcer dressings, they used jungle leaves. When they had no medicine, Weary prescribed eggs to give the sick what little nourishment he could.

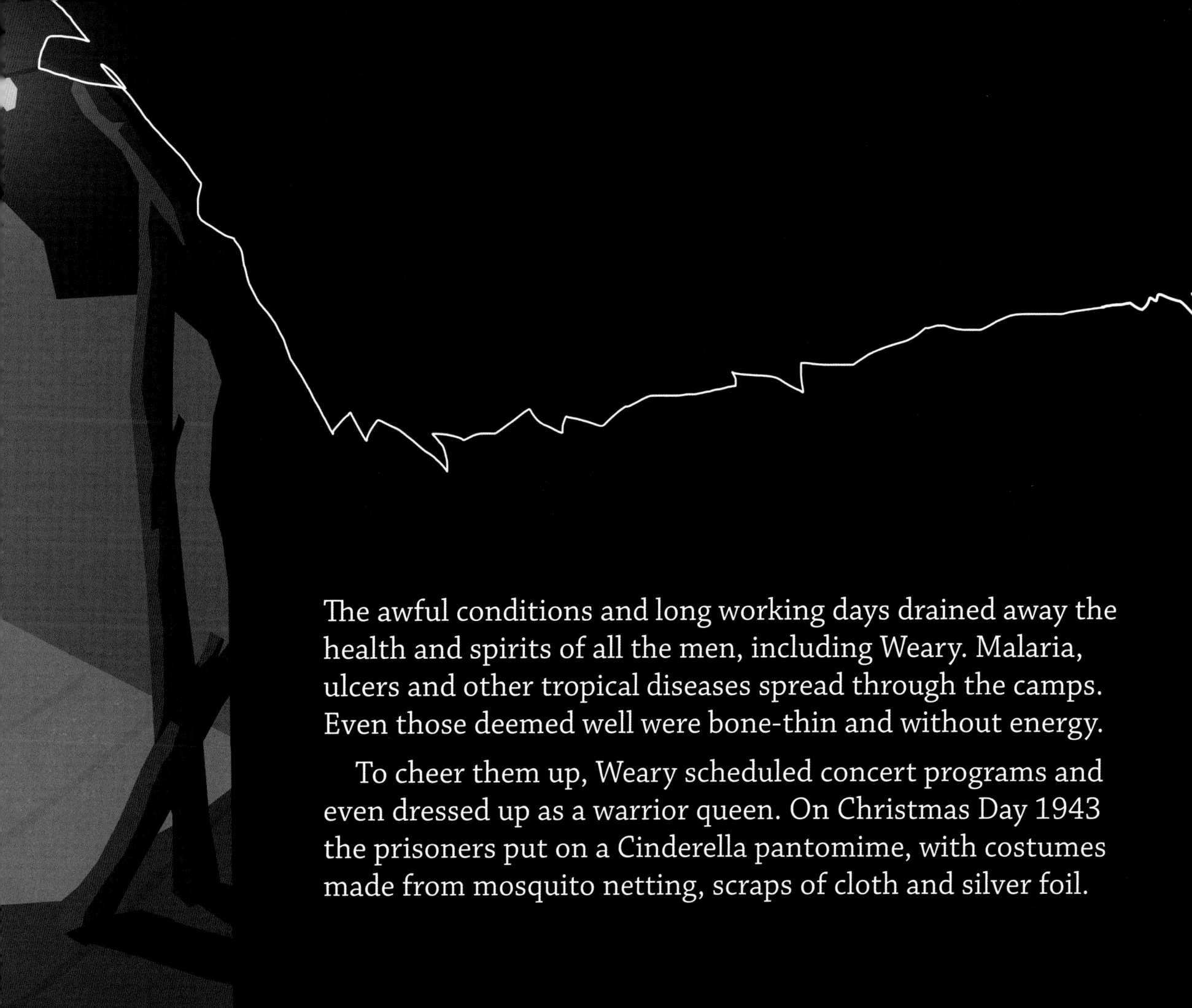

The awful conditions and long working days drained away the health and spirits of all the men, including Weary. Malaria, ulcers and other tropical diseases spread through the camps. Even those deemed well were bone-thin and without energy.

To cheer them up, Weary scheduled concert programs and even dressed up as a warrior queen. On Christmas Day 1943 the prisoners put on a Cinderella pantomime, with costumes made from mosquito netting, scraps of cloth and silver foil.

Weary tried his best to work within camp rules, but some decisions made him furious. Once, when guards refused to give him what he needed to sterilise hospital equipment, he blackened his face and hands and stole it.

When he was discovered, Weary clobbered the guard on the head, then raced back to bed and waited to be arrested. But when the guard woke up, he didn't remember a thing!

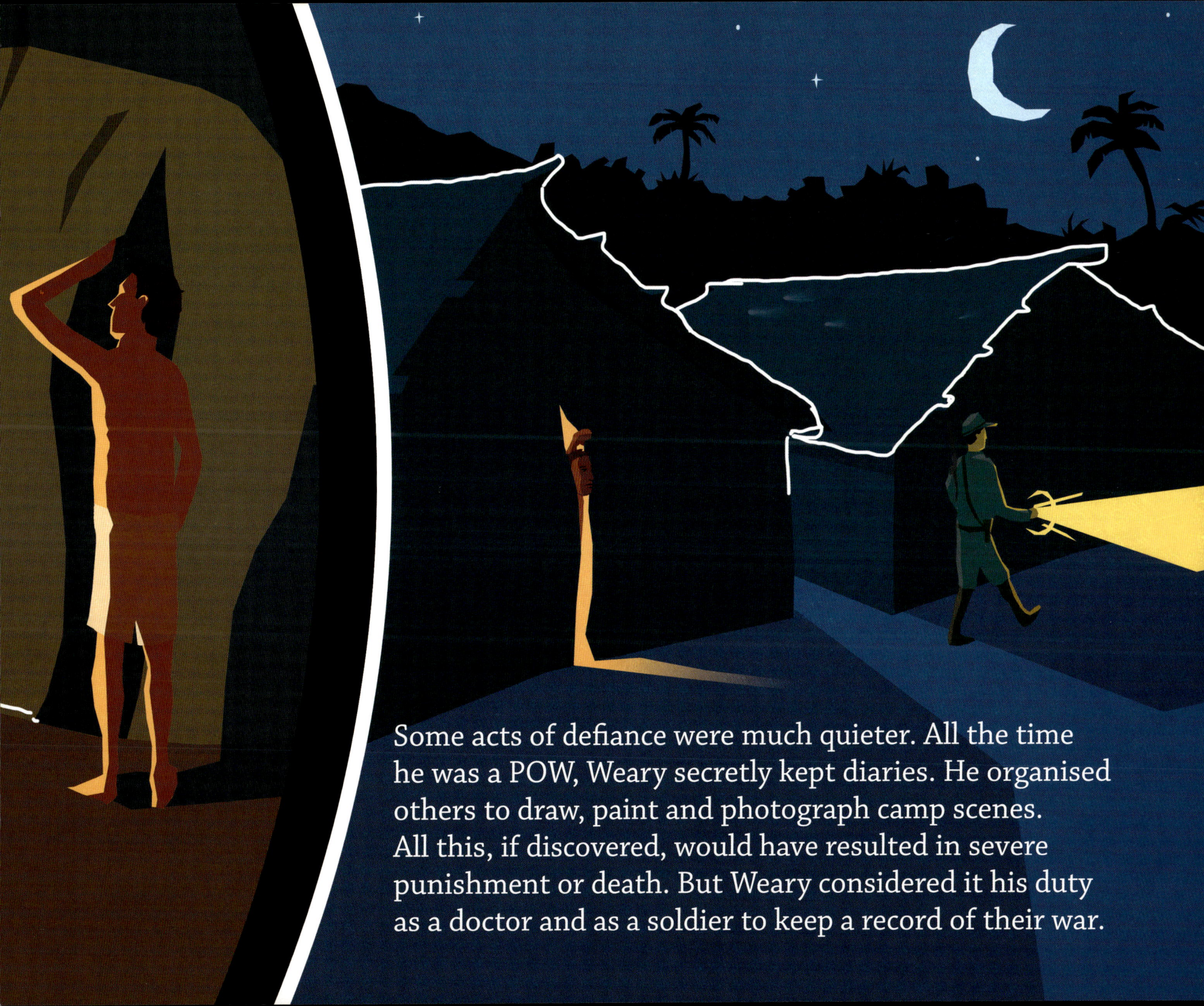

Some acts of defiance were much quieter. All the time he was a POW, Weary secretly kept diaries. He organised others to draw, paint and photograph camp scenes. All this, if discovered, would have resulted in severe punishment or death. But Weary considered it his duty as a doctor and as a soldier to keep a record of their war.

When at last the war ended in August 1945, the guards fled.
The survivors raised long-hidden flags, sang songs and cried
with relief. Weary remained in Thailand for many more weeks,
organising transport home for the sick and wounded.

Soon after, Weary was called to identify his captors. Although
he condemned what they had done, he refused to continue to hate
them. All men, he had learned, are equal in the face of suffering.

Finally, it was time to leave. Weary caught the last flight home to Australia. He had work to do, a life to live.

TIMELINE

1907 (12 July): Ernest Edward Dunlop is born at Wangaratta, in north-eastern Victoria, second son to Alice and James Dunlop.

1910: Ernest and his family move to a farm at Sheepwash Creek, between Benalla and Shepparton.

1922: The Dunlop family moves to Benalla. Ernest and his brother, Alan, attend Benalla High School. He plays tennis, football, enters diving competitions, joins cadets. At 15 years of age, he is able to lift a 95 kg wheat bag in each hand.

1924: Unsure of what to do, Ernest begins a pharmacy apprenticeship.

1927: Ernest moves to Melbourne to attend Pharmacy College.

1930: Ernest wins a scholarship to Ormond College at Melbourne University to study medicine, where he is given the nickname 'Weary'. He competes in boxing tournaments and plays rugby.

1932: Weary represents Australia at rugby.

1934: Weary graduates with first-class honours from Melbourne University.

1935: The Royal Melbourne Hospital offers Weary his first medical position, as a junior resident. He re-enlists in army reserves and is commissioned into the Australian Army Medical Corps on 1 July with the rank of Captain.

1938: In London, Weary attends St Bartholomew's Medical School and becomes a Fellow of the Royal College of Surgeons.

1939: World War II begins and Weary enlists in the Australian Army Medical Corps (6th Division). In December he is posted to Jerusalem, where he is appointed Acting Assistant Director of Medical Services.

1940 (May): Weary is promoted to Major and appointed Deputy Assistant Director of Medical Services on the staff of the Australian Corps Headquarters and AIF Headquarters in Gaza and Alexandria. He serves in both Greece and Crete.

1942: The war in the Pacific worsens and Weary is transferred to Java, Indonesia.

1942 (26 February): Weary is promoted to temporary Lt Colonel in command of No. 1 Allied General Hospital at Bandung when Java falls to the Japanese. Weary, his staff and patients are declared prisoners of war (POWs).

1942: The staff and patients are transferred to POW camps in Java and then Changi, Singapore. Weary is appointed Commander of the British and Australian prisoners.

1943 (20 January): POWs leave Singapore for Konyu River Camp, Thailand to work on the Thai–Burma Railway.

1943 (March): Weary is transferred to Hintok Mountain Camp.

1943 (October): Weary is sent to Tha Sao Hospital.

1944: Weary moves to Chungkai and then Nakom Paton.

1945 (August): The war in the Pacific ends. Weary is appointed Lt Colonel before returning home to Australia.

1945 (8 November): Helen Ferguson and Weary Dunlop marry. They go on to have two sons.

1946 (February): Weary recommences his medical career.

1969: Despite his reluctance, Weary is knighted in recognition of his contribution to medicine.

1976: Weary is declared Australian of the Year.

1988 (January): As part of bicentennial celebrations, Weary is named among 200 great Australians.

1993 (2 July): Weary dies at his home.

1993 (12 July): More than 10,000 people line the streets for Weary's state funeral, held at St Paul's Cathedral in Melbourne.